ICONIC DESIGNS

GREAT
BUILDING
DESIGNS

1900-TODAY

Ian Graham

raintree

Raintree is an imprint of Capstone Global Library Limited, a company incorporated in England and Wales having its registered office at 7 Pilgrim Street, London, EC4V 6LB – Registered company number: 6695582

www.raintree.co.uk
myorders@raintree.co.uk

Text © Capstone Global Library Limited 2016
The moral rights of the proprietor have been asserted.

Edited by Clare Lewis
Designed by Richard Parker
Original illustrations © Capstone Global Library Ltd 2015
Illustrated by HL Studios
Picture research by Jo Miller
Production by Victoria Fitzgerald
Originated by Capstone Global Library Ltd
Printed and bound in China by Leo Paper Products

ISBN 978 1 406 29672 3 (hardback)
19 18 17 16 15
10 9 8 7 6 5 4 3 2 1

ISBN 978 1 406 29677 8 (paperback)
20 19 18 17 16
10 9 8 7 6 5 4 3 2 1

British Library Cataloguing in Publication Data
A full catalogue record for this book is available from the British Library.

Acknowledgements
We would like to thank the following for permission to reproduce photographs:
Alamy: Ben Welsh Premium, 34, INTERFOTO, 11; Corbis: In Pictures/Mike Kemp, 41; DoD photo, 19; Getty Images: Hulton Archive/Keystone, 22; Internet Archives/NASA/courtesy of nasaimages.org, 21; Newscom: akg-images/Bruni Meya, 30, Everett Collection, 14, 15, UIG Universal Images Group/Mondadori Electa, 10, UPI Photo/Brian Kersey, 27, VWPics/Edwin Remsberg, 12; Shutterstock: Albo, 39, Dan Breckwoldt, 28, David Johnson, 20, denisgo, 42, Dmitry Brizhatyuk, 29, freedarst, 36, Frontpage, 17, Iakov Filimonov, 31, Ilona Ignatova, 38, InavanHateren, 24, iurii, 43, IVY PHOTOS, 8, Jorg Hackemann, 6, Kobby Dagan, 35, Malcolm Chapman, 40, Migel, 32, Philip Bird LRPS CPAGB, 37, Stuart Monk, 5, T photography, cover (inset) 9, Thomas Barrat, 26, Vadim Ratnikov, 23, Visun Khankasem, cover, 25

Design Elements Shutterstock: franco's photos, Jason Winter, URRRA

CONTENTS

Some words are shown in bold, **like this**. You can find out what they mean by looking in the glossary.

INTRODUCING ICONIC BUILDINGS

From the smallest home to the tallest **skyscraper**, people live, work and play in buildings. Every building has to be designed. Buildings are designed by **architects**. They work with engineers to turn the designs into real buildings. They often have to overcome problems such as withstanding earthquakes or saving energy. The engineers choose the materials and work out how to use them to produce a building that looks exactly like the architect's design.

WHAT iS AN iCONiC BUiLDiNG?

Iconic buildings are the most famous buildings. Some buildings are famous because of their size, their shape or the place where they were built. Iconic buildings are the stars of the architectural world, and so are the architects who designed them.

New materials

In 1900, most buildings were made from wood, bricks or stone, materials that have been used for thousands of years. After 1900, architects and engineers started using new materials such as steel and **reinforced concrete**. New materials made taller buildings and new shapes of buildings possible. Tall buildings are often built in city centres because land is expensive and in short supply. Building upwards allows a lot of floor space to be packed into a small area of land.

WORLD OF DESIGN

Architectural styles

There are different styles of buildings in the same way as there are different styles of music and clothes. Different architectural styles use different building materials, building methods and shapes of buildings. Some styles are very modern-looking. Others copy shapes that were used in the past.

Cities have a mixture of
buildings of all shapes, sizes,
ages and styles, from small
homes to giant skyscrapers.

THE FLATIRON BUILDING

FAST FACTS

Designed by: D.H. Burman and Frederick Dinkelberg
Built in: New York City, USA
Date: 1902

The Flatiron Building was designed to fit a wedge-shaped piece of land at 175 Fifth Avenue in New York City.

The Flatiron Building is famous because of its odd shape. It's called the Flatiron Building because its shape looks like an old-fashioned iron for smoothing clothes.

Its construction was made possible by a change in New York's building codes. Building codes are rules for the design and construction of buildings. They make sure that buildings are safe and strong. As building methods and materials change, building codes also change from time to time. The change in New York's building codes in 1892 allowed a steel frame to be used inside a building. A steel skeleton made it easier to design a building as tall as the 22-floor Flatiron Building.

Standing strong

Some people thought the Flatiron Building looked so thin that the wind would blow it over, but there was no danger of that because of its steel frame. The frame was made strong enough to stand up to wind four times faster than it would ever face.

WORLD OF DESIGN

Curtain walls

A building made of bricks or stone is held up by its walls. A very tall building would need very thick walls. They would be so thick that there would be no space inside for rooms. So, the walls of very tall buildings are fixed to a steel frame. The frame holds the building up so the walls can be thin. They hang on the frame like curtains, so they're called **curtain walls**.

THE EMPIRE STATE BUILDING

FAST FACTS

Designed by: William F. Lamb
Built in: New York City, USA
Date: 1931

The Empire State Building in New York City is 443 metres (1,454 feet) high. It was the first building to have more than 100 floors (it has 103).

The Empire State Building was the world's tallest building from the time of its construction in 1931 until the 1970s.

AIR CRASH

In 1945, a bomber-plane flying in fog crashed into the Empire State Building. One of its engines flew through the building and out the other side. Another engine fell down a lift shaft. One woman had an amazing escape when she survived falling 75 floors inside a lift. This is still a world record.

Art deco

The Empire State Building was designed in a style called **art deco**. Art deco was a modern design style for buildings, furniture, and all sorts of other things, and was popular from the 1920s to the 1940s. It used bold geometric shapes and colours, and lots of decoration.

Blowing a gale

The spire at the top of the Empire State Building was designed as a mooring mast for passenger **airships**. These giant aircraft flew because they were filled with hydrogen gas, making them lighter than air. However, strong winds from below blew airships about so much that they couldn't be moored safely to the mast. The winds were caused by the shape of the building and the surrounding buildings. Today, new skyscraper designs are tested to check how they affect the wind blowing around them.

The Chrysler Building is another art deco building in New York City. It was built at the same time as the Empire State Building.

VILLA SAVOYE

FAST FACTS

Designed by: Le Corbusier and Pierre Jeanneret
Built in: Poissy, France
Date: 1931

Villa Savoye is a house that was built in the **international style** of architecture. International style buildings have straight lines, smooth walls, flat roofs and no unnecessary decoration. They still look very modern even though they were built in the 1930s.

Villa Savoye was almost knocked down in the 1960s, but architects all over the world called for it to be saved because it was such an important building.

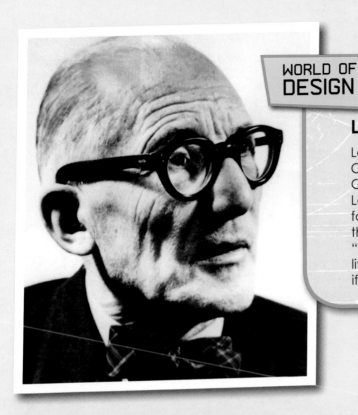

Le Corbusier

Le Corbusier's real name was Charles-Édouard Jeanneret-Gris. He started calling himself Le Corbusier in 1920 when it was fashionable for artists to give themselves new names. He said, "The house is a machine for living", so he designed houses as if they were machines.

Villa Savoye was designed by a Swiss architect called Le Corbusier and his cousin Pierre Jeanneret. It was a home for the Savoye family. It was built using reinforced concrete and it stands on thin pillars called pilotis. The pilotis open up the base of the building and make it look as if it's floating above the ground. The space can be left empty or used for parking or something else. Villa Savoye was so different from other houses being built in the 1930s that it became world famous and it made Le Corbusier famous, too.

COPYCAT BUILDINGS

Villa Savoye was so famous that copies of it were built in other countries. One of them is in Canberra, Australia. It looks like Villa Savoye except that it's black. Other architects liked the simple, unfussy style of Villa Savoye and used parts of it in their own designs for modern buildings.

FALLINGWATER

Fallingwater is a home designed by Frank Lloyd Wright for Edgar Kaufmann and his family. The family often spent time in the countryside outside Pittsburgh, USA, staying in a small cabin near a waterfall. They asked Wright to design a bigger and more permanent country home there. They thought the house would be somewhere near the waterfall, so they were surprised when they learned that Wright planned to build the house on top of the waterfall!

FAST FACTS

Designed by: Frank Lloyd Wright
Built in: Mill Run, Pennsylvania, USA
Date: 1939

Fallingwater has been open to the public since 1964. More than 4 million people have visited it.

Unusual design

Houses usually stand on a base called the **foundation**, but a normal foundation couldn't be built in the waterfall. Instead, Wright used a type of structure called a **cantilever**. The building's floors are made from reinforced concrete slabs fixed at one end to a stone chimney. Cantilevers and reinforced concrete were very unusual materials for building US homes in the 1930s, so Fallingwater quickly became famous.

Cantilevers

A cantilever is a beam or slab fixed to something at one end only, like a diving board or the wing of a plane. Anything that sticks out from the side of a building, such as a **balcony** or **veranda**, is a cantilever.

Some people thought Fallingwater wouldn't be strong enough to stand without extra supports to hold it up, but it was built exactly as Wright designed it and it did stand up. In 1991 it was voted "the best all-time work of American architecture".

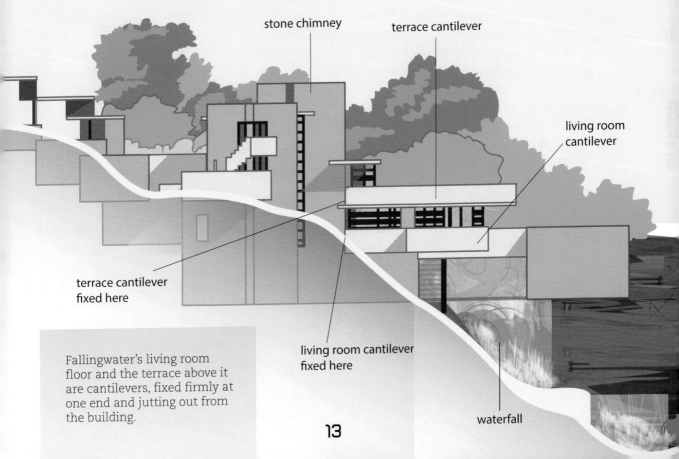

stone chimney

terrace cantilever

living room cantilever

terrace cantilever fixed here

living room cantilever fixed here

waterfall

Fallingwater's living room floor and the terrace above it are cantilevers, fixed firmly at one end and jutting out from the building.

Frank Lloyd Wright

FAST FACTS

Dates: 1867–1959
Born in: Richland Center, Wisconsin, USA
Best known for: Designing buildings in the **prairie school** style
Most iconic buildings: Fallingwater, Johnson Wax Headquarters

Frank Lloyd Wright is often called the greatest American architect. He created a building style called **organic architecture**. It means designing buildings that fit in with people and the environment. His "Fallingwater" house was the best example of this. He thought houses should fit in with the land instead of changing the land to fit the buildings. He also thought that buildings in the United States should be designed specially for the United States instead of copying old building styles from Europe.

Wright designed all sorts of buildings. As well as houses, he designed hotels, office buildings, skyscrapers, museums, schools and churches. And he designed furniture to be used inside his buildings. During his 70-year career in architecture, he produced more than 1,100 designs and nearly half of them were built. His work is often included in lists of the world's most important buildings.

The mile-high skyscraper

Frank Lloyd Wright's wildest design was a 1,600-metre (1-mile) high skyscraper. It would have been four times higher than the Empire State Building. Not all designs are built. Some are too strange-looking, too expensive or too futuristic for anyone to pay for them to be built. The mile-high skyscraper was never built.

Wright's plans for his towering mile-high skyscraper never came to reality.

The Pentagon

FAST FACTS

Place: Arlington County, Virginia, USA
Height: 23.5 metres (77 feet)
Completed: 1943
Designed by: George Bergstrom

The problem

When World War II began in 1939, the United States needed more offices to house the commanders running its military forces. Their offices were spread over the city of Washington DC in 17 different buildings. The government decided to make a new building to house them all in the same place. The US war department was growing very rapidly due to its involvement in World War II. Another building had been built earlier in the 1930s, but even before it was finished, it was clear that it wouldn't be big enough.

The concept

Architect George Bergstrom was given only three days to come up with a new design. It had to be big enough for 30,000 workers. There were some limitations on the new building. It couldn't be too tall, because most steel reserves were needed to build ships, tanks and guns for the war. There was very little left for new buildings. And the building was needed quickly.

The vast five-sided Pentagon building was built in only 16 months during World War II.

Bergstrom decided to construct a low, sprawling **concrete** building. It was designed in a five-sided shape called a pentagon, so the building quickly became known as the Pentagon. The shape was originally chosen to fit between the roads where it was to be built. Then a different location was chosen, but the pentagon shape was kept because it was too late to change it. Instead of steel elevators, Bergstrom designed concrete ramps to save on steel. There was no metal available for extra decoration so the interior of the building was very plain.

Drawings

Today, building designs are created and stored on computers. When the Pentagon was designed, large numbers of plans were drawn by hand on paper to guide the construction workers. The Pentagon had 2,500 sheets of drawings, each measuring roughly 85 centimetres by 150 centimetres (roughly 3 feet by 5 feet).

The build

The Pentagon was built in record time between 1941 and 1943 using 15,000 workers. At one point, engineers and builders were working through the night to get it finished. Construction was so fast that some parts were built before proper plans were even drawn.

The ground on which it was built was originally swamp land. Huge amounts of earth had to be brought in to make the ground more solid. Workers took sand and gravel from the nearby Potomac River. This was also used to make the huge amounts of concrete needed in the build.

The first workers moved into their offices in the Pentagon before the building was even complete.

Improvements

By 1994, it was clear that the Pentagon was in need of modernization. Work began on major improvements. Many of the ramps were replaced by new lifts. Work was done to better equip the offices with modern technology, while safety features were improved.

Tragedy at the Pentagon

On 11 September, 2001, just as the improvement work was coming to an end, hijackers deliberately flew a passenger aeroplane into the Pentagon. Nearly 200 people died, both passengers on the plane and workers inside the Pentagon. In 2008, a memorial garden at the Pentagon was opened in memory of those who died. The renovation work continued and was finally finished in 2013.

The people who lost their lives on September 11, 2001, are now commemorated at this memorial at the Pentagon.

Pentagon today

Today, the Pentagon is still a symbol of US military power. It remains one of the biggest office buildings in the world.

Pentagon facts

- The Pentagon has five floors above ground and two floors below ground.
- There are 27 kilometres (17 miles) of corridors.
- Up to 25,000 people work at the Pentagon.
- It has more office space than two Empire State Buildings.
- It takes seven minutes to walk between any two pentagon points in the building.
- For those unable to walk the large distances in the building, scooters are provided.

THE VEHICLE ASSEMBLY BUILDING, KENNEDY SPACE CENTER

The Vehicle Assembly Building (VAB) has been used for building manned space vehicles at the Kennedy Space Center in Florida, USA, since 1968. It had to be big enough to hold the giant *Saturn V* Moon rockets.

FAST FACTS

Designed by: Max O. Urbahn
Built in: Kennedy Space Center, Florida, USA
Date: 1965

NASA's Vehicle Assembly Building is as tall as a 52-floor skyscraper.

World's biggest doors

With an *Apollo* spacecraft on top, a *Saturn V* rocket stood 111 metres (363 feet) high. The VAB's doors were made tall enough for one of these rockets to pass through standing on top of its launch platform. They're the biggest doors in the world!

The building stands 160 metres (525 feet) high. Inside, it's almost as big as four Empire State Buildings. After the *Apollo* spaceflights to the Moon ended in the 1970s, the building was used to assemble **Space Shuttles** just before they were launched. After the last Space Shuttle flight in 2011, work began to prepare the building to handle a new generation of rockets.

Storm force

Florida is often hit by violent storms and hurricanes, so the VAB had to be made strong enough to withstand some of the world's strongest winds. The building is fixed to the ground by 4,225 steel pipes that go down 50 metres (164 feet) into the rock below the building.

IT'S RAINING ... INSIDE!

The VAB is so big that it creates its own weather inside the building. Rain-clouds can form high up under the roof. To stop this from happening, the air inside the building is continually pumped out and replaced with fresh air.

Sydney Opera House

FAST FACTS

Place: Sydney, Australia
Height: 67 metres (221 feet)
Completed: 1973
Designed by: Jørn Utzon

The best design

In 1954, the government of the Australian state of New South Wales wanted to build a new opera house. It held a competition to find the best design. There were 233 entries from 28 countries. The winner was a Danish architect called Jørn Utzon.

Jørn Utzon was inspired by the work of earlier architects, including Frank Lloyd Wright.

Utzon's design for the new Sydney Opera House showed a set of interlocking sail-like shells. They were to be built on top of a platform called the **podium** on the shore of Sydney Harbour.

Building the podium

The podium sits on hundreds of concrete blocks called **piers**. Each pier is 1 metre (3 feet) across. The piers support the weight of the podium and the building on top of it, and stop them from sinking into the mud.

Reinforced concrete can be made into almost any shape an architect can think of.

Building the shells

When the podium was finished, work could begin on the shells that form the building. These were made from concrete and lifted up into position by cranes. The tallest shells reach a height of 67 metres (221 feet). The tower cranes that lifted them were the biggest in the world at that time.

Reinforced concrete

Concrete is very strong if it's squashed, but it breaks easily if it's bent or stretched. The concrete used in skyscrapers and the Sydney Opera House is strengthened by pouring it over steel rods called **rebars**. When it sets hard, the rebars make it stronger. This is called reinforced concrete.

Tiling the roof

Sydney Opera House gleams in the sunshine, because its concrete structure is covered with cream and white tiles. The tiles were specially designed for the building. They are covered with a layer of crushed stone so that they glisten in bright sunshine without making dazzling, blinding reflections.

WORLD OF DESIGN

It took three years to produce the tiles that made the Sydney Opera House look exactly as Jørn Utzon wanted it to look.

Computer aided design

The Sydney Opera House was one of the first buildings to be designed with the help of computers. Engineers had to work out if it was strong enough to stand up under its own weight. It was such a strange shape that thousands of difficult sums had to be done to find the answer. Computers could do them much faster than people.

Inside the building

Utzon's design for the inside of the building was turned down, because it was too expensive. He disagreed with the newly elected government of New South Wales in 1965 and resigned the following year. A new team finished the inside. It houses a 2,679-seat concert hall, a 1,507-seat theatre and several smaller theatres and performance spaces. Sydney Opera House finally opened in 1973. In 1999, Utzon helped to write a set of rules for future work and alterations to the building. He died in 2008.

There is no other building like the Sydney Opera House anywhere in the world.

Sydney Opera House facts

- Every year, more than 8 million people visit Sydney Opera House.
- Ten thousand builders worked on its construction.
- It is covered with more than 1 million tiles.

THE WILLIS TOWER

FAST FACTS

Designed by: Skidmore, Owings and Merrill
Built in: Chicago, USA
Date: 1973

The Willis Tower was the world's tallest building for more than 20 years. It has towered over Chicago since 1973. Its 108 floors reach a height of 442 metres (1,450 feet). It used to be called the Sears Tower and lots of people still call it the Sears Tower.

The Willis Tower took 2,000 workers three years to build.

You can see four US states (Illinois, Indiana, Wisconsin and Michigan) from the top of the Willis Tower on a clear day.

It was designed as a bundle of nine square tubes standing on end, giving the building its "boxy" look. This type of skyscraper design, known as a bundled tube structure, was invented by Fazlur Rahman Khan. The Willis Tower was the first skyscraper to use it.

The building is full of offices where people work, but one floor is kept for visitors who want to see the great view from the top. They can go to the Skydeck on the 103rd floor and look out across Chicago and beyond. More than 1.5 million people visit the Skydeck every year.

GLASS FLOOR

In 2009, four glass balconies were added to the Skydeck. They stick out from the side of the building. Brave visitors can stand in them and look down through the glass floor to the ground 412 metres (1,353 feet) below their feet! The glass is 1.3 centimetres (half an inch) thick and is strong enough to hold a weight of 5 tonnes.

THE LLOYD'S BUILDING

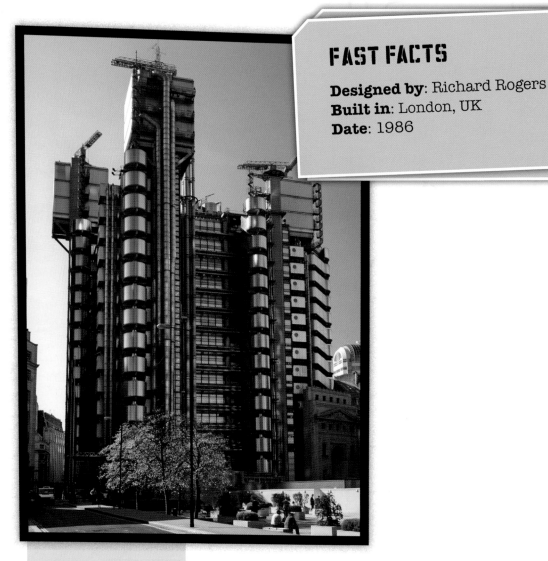

The inside-out Lloyd's Building in London is covered with gleaming **stainless steel**.

The Lloyd's Building in London is an example of a building style called **hi-tech**. All large modern buildings have lifts, pipes and machinery that are usually hidden inside the building. The Lloyd's Building was designed to have all of this equipment and machinery on the outside. Putting them on the outside leaves more space inside the building for offices and workers. The Lloyd's Building is sometimes called the Inside-Out Building, because of its unusual design and appearance.

Space craft

The Lloyd's Building is made of six towers with a big open hall called an **atrium** in the middle. The atrium is 76 metres (249 feet) high. Sunlight floods into it through a glass roof. People work in offices on 14 floors around the sides of the atrium. Walls can be placed anywhere in the offices to divide up the space in any way the workers choose.

THE POMPIDOU CENTRE

The Pompidou Centre in Paris, France, is another famous hi-tech, inside-out building. It houses a vast public library and a museum of modern art. It was designed by Renzo Piano, Richard Rogers and Gianfranco Francini. It opened in 1977 and was named after a former president of France.

The pipes and machinery outside the Pompidou Centre are painted in different colours that show what they do. Water pipes are green, air pipes are blue and so on.

Richard Rogers

FAST FACTS

Dates: Born 23 July, 1933
Born in: Florence, Italy
Best known for: hi-tech buildings
Most iconic buildings: The Pompidou Centre, Paris; The Lloyd's Building, London; The Millennium Dome, London

Richard Rogers was born in 1933 in Italy. During World War II, his family moved to England. He studied architecture in London and at Yale University in the United States. Then he returned to the United Kingdom and started his own company with other architects.

He quickly became known for hi-tech "inside-out" buildings that had all of their pipes and machinery on the outside. Some of his buildings looked so unusual that at first some people disliked them, but then they got used to them and finally even liked them.

Richard Rogers is one of the most famous British architects.

Rogers has designed all sorts of buildings, including airport terminals, shopping centres, government buildings, law courts, office buildings and factories. He has won a lot of prizes and awards for his work. In 1996, he was made Baron Rogers of Riverside by Queen Elizabeth II.

Moody buildings

Architects like Richard Rogers know that the shape, size and colour of the spaces inside a building can affect the way visitors to the building feel. Rogers designed a passenger building at Barajas Airport in Madrid, Spain, to take the worry out of catching a flight. There is a lot of space and light inside, and it's easy for people to find their way through the building.

Terminal 4 at Madrid's Barajas Airport, designed by Richard Rogers, won one of the most important prizes in architecture, the Stirling Prize.

THE PETRONAS TOWERS

FAST FACTS

Designed by: César Pelli
Built in: Kuala Lumpur, Malaysia
Date: 1996

When the Petronas Towers were built, they were the world's tallest buildings. The two towers are 452 metres (1,483 feet) high. When engineers tested the ground they found that it wasn't strong enough to hold the building's weight, so instead it was built 61 metres (200 feet) away, where the ground was stronger.

It takes window cleaners a month to wash all of the Petronas Towers' 32,000 windows.

If you could cut through one of the Petronas Towers, you would find that it is the shape of an eight-pointed star called a Rub el Hizb.

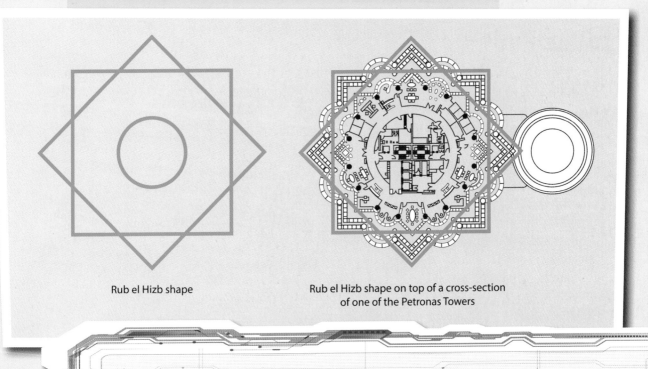

Rub el Hizb shape

Rub el Hizb shape on top of a cross-section of one of the Petronas Towers

IDEAS FOR SHAPES

When architects design buildings, they often think about the shapes that are already in the city or country where the building will be. The Petronas Towers were built in Malaysia, where most people are Muslim. The idea for the shape of the towers came from a Muslim symbol called a Rub el Hizb.

The towers are connected by a bridge called a skybridge. The skybridge lets people cross from one tower to the other without having to go all the way down to the ground. Tall buildings sway a little when the wind blows. The skybridge is designed to slide in and out of the towers so that it doesn't break when the towers move.

WORLD OF DESIGN

Piles

Tall buildings stand on underground legs called piles. The piles usually stand on solid rock, called bedrock. The rock under the Petronas Towers is quite a long way down below them, so piles up to 115 metres (380 feet) long had to be used to reach the rock.

33

THE GUGGENHEIM MUSEUM, BILBAO

When the members of the Guggenheim Foundation decided to build a museum in Bilbao, Spain, they wanted something daring and different. They chose a Canadian-American architect called Frank Gehry to design it. His buildings look very modern. They are often strange shapes and have walls standing at unusual angles.

FAST FACTS

Designed by: Frank Gehry
Built in: Bilbao, Spain
Date: 1997

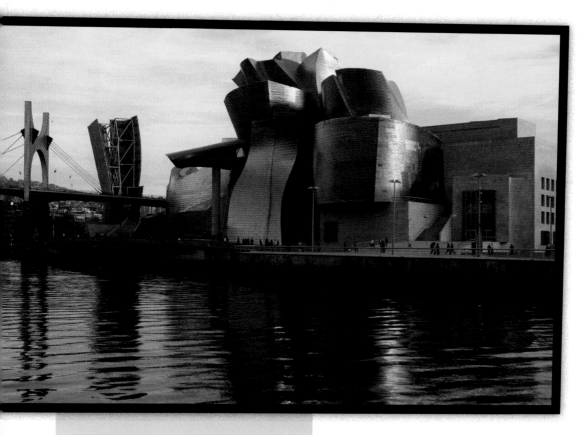

The Guggenheim Museum in Bilbao is such a strange shape that computer programs normally used for designing aircraft were used to help design it.

Form and function

The shape of most buildings is chosen to match what the building will be used for. That's why schools, shops and office buildings usually look different from each other. It's known as "form follows function". But you can't tell what a Frank Gehry building is just by looking at it. Form doesn't follow function. It's a style called **deconstructivism**.

For Bilbao, Gehry designed a building with curved walls covered on the outside with 33,000 shiny metal sheets. He chose titanium for this. Titanium is a very strong metal that is lightweight and doesn't rust. The metal sheets look a bit like fish scales. Inside, the curving walls make 20 galleries for showing paintings, sculptures and other works of art.

Gehry's Guggenheim Museum in Bilbao was a great success. Lots of people loved it because of its amazing shape and appearance. It quickly became so famous that thousands of people travelled to Bilbao just to see it and would then spend a holiday in the city. Because of this, the way a new building can bring more visitors to a city is now called the Bilbao Effect.

Gehry used similar curved shapes when he designed the Cleveland Clinic Building in Las Vegas, USA.

KHAN SHATYR

Khan Shatyr in Astana, Kazakhstan is the world's biggest tent. It was designed and built by a team of architects and engineers led by Norman Foster. The 150-metre (500-feet) high tent is made from self-cleaning plastic held up by **cables** hanging from a tall spire. The spire stands on top of three giant tubular-steel legs.

The shape of Khan Shatyr was inspired by one of the oldest types of homes used in Kazakhstan, called a yurt.

Strong and light

The roof has to withstand temperatures as low as -35 degrees Celsius (-31 degrees Fahrenheit) in winter and as high as 35 degrees Celsius (95 degrees Fahrenheit) in summer. It is designed to be light and flexible. It moves when the wind blows against it and yet it is strong enough to withstand the weight of heavy winter snowfalls. It also lets sunlight pass through. There is enough space inside for 10,000 people. While they're inside, visitors can enjoy a giant indoor park with a jogging track, a tropical beach and an amusement park.

THE MILLENNIUM DOME

The Millennium Dome, now called the O2, in London was built to mark the turn of the millennium, in the year 2000. Like Khan Shatyr, it's a dome-shaped tent stretched over a net of steel cables. The cables hang from 12 towers representing the months of the year. The dome is 52 metres (170 feet) high, representing the weeks of the year, and 365 metres (1,197 feet) across, representing the days of the year.

The roof of the Millennium Dome is so light that it actually weighs less than the air inside the dome!

BURJ KHALIFA

Burj Khalifa is the world's tallest skyscraper. It stands an astonishing 828 metres (2,716 feet) high. That's about twice the height of the Empire State Building, which was itself once the tallest building in the world. The shape of the building was carefully designed to stop it from twisting in the wind. It's also thinner at the top to reduce the building's weight.

It was built from reinforced concrete, which makes it stronger than a skyscraper with a steel frame. Specially hard concrete was used at the bottom to support the huge weight pressing down from above. It stands on nearly 200 underground legs called piles, which hold it upright. The towering building is covered with 26,000 glass panels and gleaming stainless steel. Construction began in 2004 and was completed in 2010.

Burj Khalifa's 163 floors are divided into homes, offices, a restaurant and a hotel. People travel up and down the building using 57 lifts and 8 escalators.

FAST FACTS

Designed by: Adrian Smith
Built in: Dubai, United Arab Emirates
Date: 2010

The Transamerica Pyramid in San Francisco is a modern building that was inspired by one of the oldest structures – the pyramid.

DIFFERENT SHAPES

In the 1960s, architects thought about using new shapes for buildings instead of the usual box-shaped blocks. William Pereira, an American architect, designed a building called the Transamerica **Pyramid** in San Francisco, USA. It was completed in 1972. Its pyramid shape lets more sunlight reach the ground around the building. The "wings" on each side have lifts and stairs inside.

THE SHARD

The Shard is the tallest building in Western Europe. It soars to a height of 310 metres (1,017 feet). The idea for its shape came from the church spires and ships' masts that were seen along the River Thames in past centuries.

The Shard's designer, Renzo Piano, described the giant building as a vertical city for thousands of people.

Hanging around

The Shard's workers needed a good head for heights. The last pieces at the top of the building were fitted by workers hanging from ropes. Some of the 11,000 sheets of glass that cover the building have to be cleaned in the same way, by workers dangling from ropes!

STEEL OR CONCRETE?

Parts of the Shard have a steel frame inside and other parts have concrete inside. The floors used as offices have a steel frame, because this leaves lots of space inside for offices. The floors where people live are made of concrete, because concrete is better at stopping noise spreading from one home to another.

The "walkie talkie" building reflected sunlight like a giant curved mirror, causing problems on the ground nearby.

WORLD OF DESIGN

Design dangers

A new skyscraper at 20 Fenchurch Street, London, melted part of a car because of its unusual shape! The building, nicknamed the "walkie-talkie", has curved glass walls. They focused sunlight like a curved mirror onto a car parked below the building. The heat melted part of the car! The problem was solved by fitting the building with a sunshade made of metal fins running across the building to deflect the sunlight.

THE FUTURE OF BUILDING DESIGN

Architects will carry on pushing the limits of what is possible in building design. They are already designing the buildings that will amaze us in the future. There are designs for even taller buildings than the tallest today, new shapes of buildings and even buildings that change shape!

The buildings in future cities might be very different from buildings today.

Some of the strangest designs for future skyscrapers have floors that slowly rotate. If you were to live in a building like this, the view through your window would change from day to day. Architects are planning to build some skyscrapers that are taller than 1 kilometre (3,280 feet). They include the Mubarak al-Kabir Tower in Kuwait, the Murjan Tower in Bahrain and the Azerbaijan Tower in Baku, Azerbaijan.

Design a building

If you were to design a building, what would it be like? Would it be a home or a factory or an office building? Would it be a skyscraper? What would it be made of? What shape would it be? It has to work as a building, so where would the rooms, stairs and entrance be?

Green buildings

Future buildings will be kinder to the environment, or "greener", by using less electricity. Some of these buildings will produce some of the electricity they need by using **solar panels** or **wind turbines**. Solar panels make electricity from sunlight. Wind turbines make electricity when the wind blows. Some future buildings might be warmed by taking heat from the ground underneath them. And they will save rainwater for cleaning and cooling the building.

How would you like to live or work in an amazing building like this? One day you might have the chance.

TIMELINE

1902 The Flatiron Building becomes one of the first buildings in New York City to be built around a steel frame

1931 The Empire State Building in New York City is completed, becoming the world's tallest building

1931 The Swiss architect Le Corbusier and his cousin Pierre Jeanneret design Villa Savoye

1939 The American architect Frank Lloyd Wright builds a house called Fallingwater on top of a waterfall

1943 The Pentagon, still one of the biggest office buildings in the world, is built to house US military commanders and planners during World War II

1945 A bomber flying in fog crashes into the Empire State Building

1954 The Australian state of New South Wales holds a competition to find the best design for a new opera house in Sydney. The winner is a Danish architect, Jørn Utzon.

1965 The Vehicle Assembly Building is constructed at the Kennedy Space Center to assemble giant *Saturn V* rockets

1973 Jørn Utzon's unique Sydney Opera House finally opens for business after 14 years of construction work

1973 The Sears Tower opens in Chicago after three years of construction work, becoming the world's tallest building. In 2009, it is renamed the Willis Tower.

1977 The Pompidou Centre in Paris is completed, six years after the architects Renzo Piano and Richard Rogers won an international competition to design it

1986 The Lloyd's building surprises Londoners with its inside-out design

1991 Fallingwater is voted "the best all-time work of American architecture"

1996 The Petronas Towers in Kuala Lumpur, Malaysia, are together the tallest building in the world, the first skyscraper outside the United States to hold this record

1997 The Guggenheim Museum, Bilbao, wows visitors with its unusual design

1999 The Millennium Dome, London, a giant tent, celebrates the arrival of the new millennium

2009 Four glass balconies are added to the Skydeck on the 103rd floor of the Willis Tower

2010 Burj Khalifa, in the desert kingdom of Dubai, smashes all height records for buildings, standing 828 metres (2,716 feet) high

GLOSSARY

airship aircraft that produces lift using trapped gases lighter than air and which is moved along using propellers

architect someone who designs buildings

art deco design style from the 1920s and 1930s that uses strong geometrical shapes and bold colours

atrium large central hall or space in a building, usually with a glass roof

balcony platform or gallery that sticks out from the wall of a building, surrounded by a handrail or wall

cable strong, thick rope or metal wire for pulling or lifting, or a bundle of electrical wires wound together

cantilever beam held at one end only

concrete mixture of sand, cement, gravel (or broken stone) and water that sets as hard as rock, used to construct buildings

curtain wall outside wall that does not support a building's weight

deconstructivism style of architecture that uses strange shapes and walls standing at odd angles

foundation lowest part of a building, the part that holds the building up and stops it from toppling over

hi-tech style of architecture that uses the structure and machinery of the building as part of the design

international style style of modern architecture with straight lines, smooth walls, flat roofs and no unnecessary decoration

NASA National Aeronautics and Space Administration, the organization that runs US non-military space missions and carries out research with aircraft and spacecraft

organic architecture style of architecture that produces buildings that fit in with the land instead of changing the land to fit the buildings

pier deck built over water or, in architecture, a pillar-like structure that supports part of a bridge or building

podium wall or platform that forms the base of a building

prairie school style of architecture with low, wide buildings, inspired by the prairies of the American Midwest. Prairies are large areas of treeless grassland in the United States and Canada.

pyramid giant stone structure with a square base and triangular sides meeting at the top, built as a tomb in ancient Egypt

rebar reinforcement bar, a steel rod embedded in concrete to strengthen it

reinforced concrete concrete made with steel rods called rebars inside it to make it stronger

skyscraper tall building containing offices or homes

solar panel sheet of material that changes sunlight into electricity

Space Shuttle manned spacecraft with wings that could be launched again and again. A fleet of US Space Shuttles carried astronauts and cargo between Earth and space from 1981 to 2011.

stainless steel type of steel that does not rust

veranda gallery, platform or balcony with a roof along the outside wall of a building

wind turbine machine with long, wing-like blades turned by the wind to produce electricity

FIND OUT MORE

Books

13 Buildings Children Should Know, Annette Roeder (Prestel, 2009)

From Mud Huts to Skyscrapers: Architecture for Children, Christine Paxmann (Prestel, 2012)

See Inside Famous Buildings, Rob Lloyd Jones (Usborne, 2009)

The Picture History of Great Buildings, Gillian Clements (Frances Lincoln Children's Books, 2011)

The World's Most Amazing Skyscrapers (Landmark Top Tens), Michael Hurley (Raintree, 2011)

DVDs

Building Big: Skyscrapers
Produced by Wgbh/PBS, 2004, 1 disc, 60 minutes. This US DVD deals with the history, design and construction of skyscrapers.

Super Skyscrapers
Produced by PBS, 2014, 2 discs, 240 minutes. A US DVD of four PBS television programmes telling the stories of four modern skyscrapers – One World Trade Centre and One57 in New York, the Shanghai Tower in China and The Leadenhall Building in London.

Websites

science.howstuffworks.com/engineering/structural/skyscraper.htm
If you want to know how skyscrapers are built, how they stand up and why the wind doesn't blow them over, then this is the website for you.

www.australia.gov.au/about-australia/australian-story/sydney-opera-house
You can read the whole story of Sydney Opera House here – its history, the design, the materials used, how it was built and how it is used.

www.pbs.org/wgbh/buildingbig/skyscraper/basics.html
This web page looks at tall buildings through the ages, with links to more pages about skyscrapers, including a quiz to test your skyscraper knowledge.

www.sciencekids.co.nz/sciencefacts/engineering/empirestatebuilding.html
On this website, you'll find some interesting facts about the Empire State Building, from the number of times it's struck by lightning every year to how many workers built it.

Places to Visit

The View at the Shard
32 London Bridge Street,
Southwark, London. SE1 9SG
Tel: 0844 499 7111
Website:
www.the-shard.com/the-view-from-the-shard
Email:
enquiries@theviewfromtheshard.com
Three floors at the top of Western Europe's
tallest building, The Shard in London, are
open to the public, giving amazing views
across London. They're called The View
at the Shard. You'll need a ticket to get in
and The Shard recommend that you book
ahead before you visit.

Victoria & Albert Museum
Cromwell Road, London. SW7 2RL
Tel: 020 7942 2000
Website: www.vam.ac.uk
Email: vanda@vam.ac.uk
In 2004, the V & A, the world's greatest
museum of art and design, opened the
first museum gallery in the UK dedicated
to British architecture.

Design Museum
Shad Thames, London. SE1 2YD
Tel: 020 7403 6933
Website: www.designmuseum.org
Email: info@designmuseum.org
The Design Museum has a collection of
thousands of objects showing the key
designs that shaped the modern world. Its
exhibitions are constantly changing and
some of these are devoted to architectural
design.

Ideas for research

Some people have suggested using some skyscrapers in cities as vertical farms. They
would be full of food crops instead of offices or homes. Do you think this would work?
Why would farmers want to grow crops high above the ground? Think about the
distances food is transported from farms to cities and the number of trucks needed.

Think about your own home and how it is designed. Does the design work well or can you
think of ways to improve it? Would you change the shape or size of your home, or change
the numbers of rooms? Would you make it from different materials? Would you move
the kitchen or the bathroom to a different place? Would you make the windows bigger or
smaller?

Most scientists think that the world is warming up and that this is changing our weather,
making storms, floods and droughts more common. How might you change buildings, or
where they are built, to cope with more extreme weather? In low-lying countries like The
Netherlands, floating homes have been built on land that often floods. When the water
rises, the home floats instead of being flooded.